P9-BYY-644

the man who

HEYER SCHOOL LIBRARY
629.45 SCH
The man who went to the far
30118010076812

went to the

THE STORY OF
APOLLO 11 ASTRONAUT
MICHAEL COLLINS

far side of
the moon

BY BEA UUSMA SCHYFFERT

chronicle books · san francisco

WAUKES   ARY SCHOOL

...I'M GOING TO STEP OFF THE LM NOW...

Astronaut Neil Armstrong's heart is beating 156 times per minute as he lands the lunar module on the moon with only 45 seconds left of fuel. He opens the hatch. He climbs down the ladder, slowly. One-fifth of the Earth's population are sitting in front of their TV sets, holding their breath, as Neil Armstrong carefully sets the first footprint in the lunar dust.

Meanwhile—on the other side of the moon—a small spacecraft orbits in the darkness. Inside the silvery craft sits Michael Collins. He will never walk on the moon. His task is to maneuver the capsule and wait while Neil Armstrong and Buzz Aldrin land the lunar module. He can't even hear Neil and Buzz over the radio. No one is farther away from Earth than he is. For 14 lonely turns, Michael Collins circles the moon. Each time he reaches the far side of the moon he spends 48 minutes without radio communication. The only thing between him and outer space is some insulation and a thin sheet of metal.

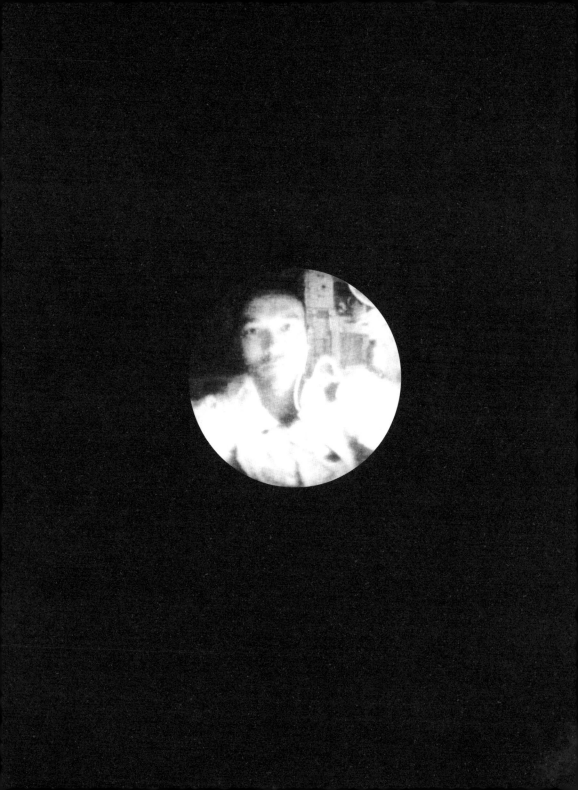

As he disappears into the shadow of the far side of the moon, Michael Collins thinks to himself that he sees a new color. The darkness outside the windows of the capsule can't be described by any earthly name. "Black" is not enough. Because there is no light, he can no longer see the surface of the moon, but he knows it's there because in that part of the sky there are no stars. They are blocked by the moon.

Circling the moon, turn after turn, he waits for Neil and Buzz to finish up down there. The windows of the capsule have misted over. The walls are squeaking a little. He has brought a camera. He takes pictures of his stubbled face. He talks into a tape recorder. He thinks about his family. He says his children's names aloud, slowly. Kate. Ann. Michael.

Ann, Michael Jr., Michael, Pat, Kate, and Dubhe (named after a star)

I am alone now, truly alone,
and absolutely isolated from
any known life. I am it.

If a count were taken, the score
would be three billion plus two
over on the other side of the moon,
and one plus God only knows what
on this side. I feel this powerfully
—not as fear or loneliness — but as
awareness, anticipation, satisfaction,
confidence, almost exultation.

I like the feeling.

Michael Collins

Before Neil and Buzz can take off from the moon and return to the capsule, Michael has to make 850 computer commands. Surrounding him on the walls of the capsule are more than 700 switches, levers, alarm buttons, gauges, warning lights, and computer keys. There are sensors that should never, *ever,* point to red. There are yellow-and-black-striped buttons with functions so important that they are covered with plastic lids to prevent a tired, lonely astronaut from pushing them by mistake.

The president calls Neil and Buzz on the moon. No one calls Michael. When he is on the far side of the moon, radio transmission from Earth is not even possible.

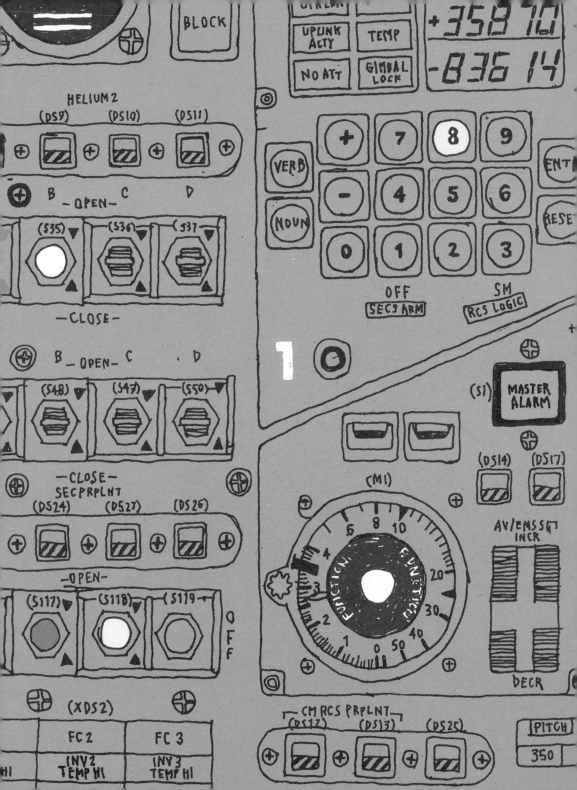

to the moon

It is July 16, 1969. A Wednesday. Although it is only half past nine in the morning, it is already 86°F (30°C) outside. One million people have gathered at Kennedy Space Center in Florida. There are people as far as the eye can see, sitting beside their campers and tents, scattered among the dunes, on picnic blankets and folding chairs. Many are still stuck in traffic on the highway.

The rocket *Saturn 5* is standing on Launch Pad 39A. It is the largest rocket ever built. It is larger than a football field set on end. In the very top of the rocket, inside the spacecraft, three astronauts are securely fastened in their seats. So far, 23 American astronauts and 17 Soviet cosmonauts have been sent into space, but this is the first time anyone will try to land on the moon. For more than 10 years, the United States and the Soviet Union have been racing to see who will get there first.

Michael Collins, Buzz Aldrin, and Neil Armstrong have written farewell letters to their wives and children. The envelopes will be opened only if the astronauts do not return.

ASTRONAUT

MICHAEL COLLINS

COMMAND MODULE PILOT
APOLLO 11

ASSIGNMENT:

EXCEPT DURING TAKEOFF, MICHAEL WILL NAVIGATE THE SPACECRAFT *COLUMBIA*.

HE IS THE ONLY ASTRONAUT ON THE TRIP WHO WILL NOT STEP ONTO THE MOON.

HE WILL CIRCLE THE MOON IN THE CAPSULE WHILE NEIL AND BUZZ LAND THE LUNAR MODULE *EAGLE* ON THE MOON.

IF THE LUNAR MODULE FAILS TO LIFT OFF FROM THE MOON, HE WILL HAVE TO PILOT THE COMMAND MODULE BACK TO EARTH BY HIMSELF.

BACKGROUND:

WORKED AS A USAF TEST PILOT BEFORE BEING SELECTED FOR NASA ASTRONAUT TRAINING.

4,000 HOURS OF FLYING TIME.

BORN IN ROME, ITALY.

FATHER WAS A MAJOR GENERAL IN THE USAF.

GREW UP ON MILITARY BASES ALL OVER THE WORLD.

MISCELLANEOUS:

DESCRIBES HIMSELF AS A NON-TECHNICAL PERSON: "HERE I AM, A FANCY HEAVY-EQUIPMENT OPERATOR WHO COULDN'T FIX ANY PIECE OF THIS MACHINE IF IT BROKE. EVEN MY WIFE IS A BETTER MECHANIC THAN I."

STUBBORN. EFFICIENT. GETS THINGS DONE.

A MAN OF FEW WORDS.

INTERESTED IN FINE WINE.

LIKES TO FISH.

PAINTS.

ENJOYS GROWING ROSES.

AGE:
38 YEARS

MARRIED TO:
PATRICIA
(FORMERLY EMPLOYED BY THE USAF WELFARE CORPS)

PETS: **DUBHE**
(GERMAN SHEPHERD)
SNOWBALL (RABBIT)

BORN:
OCTOBER 31, 1930

SALARY:
$17,147 PER YEAR

HEIGHT:
5 FEET, 11 INCHES
(180 CENTIMETERS)

CHILDREN:
KATHLEEN, 10
ANN, 7
MICHAEL JR., 6

ASTRONAUT SINCE:
1963

WEIGHT:
165 POUNDS
(75 KILOGRAMS)

PREVIOUS SPACE TRAVEL:
GEMINI 10, 1966

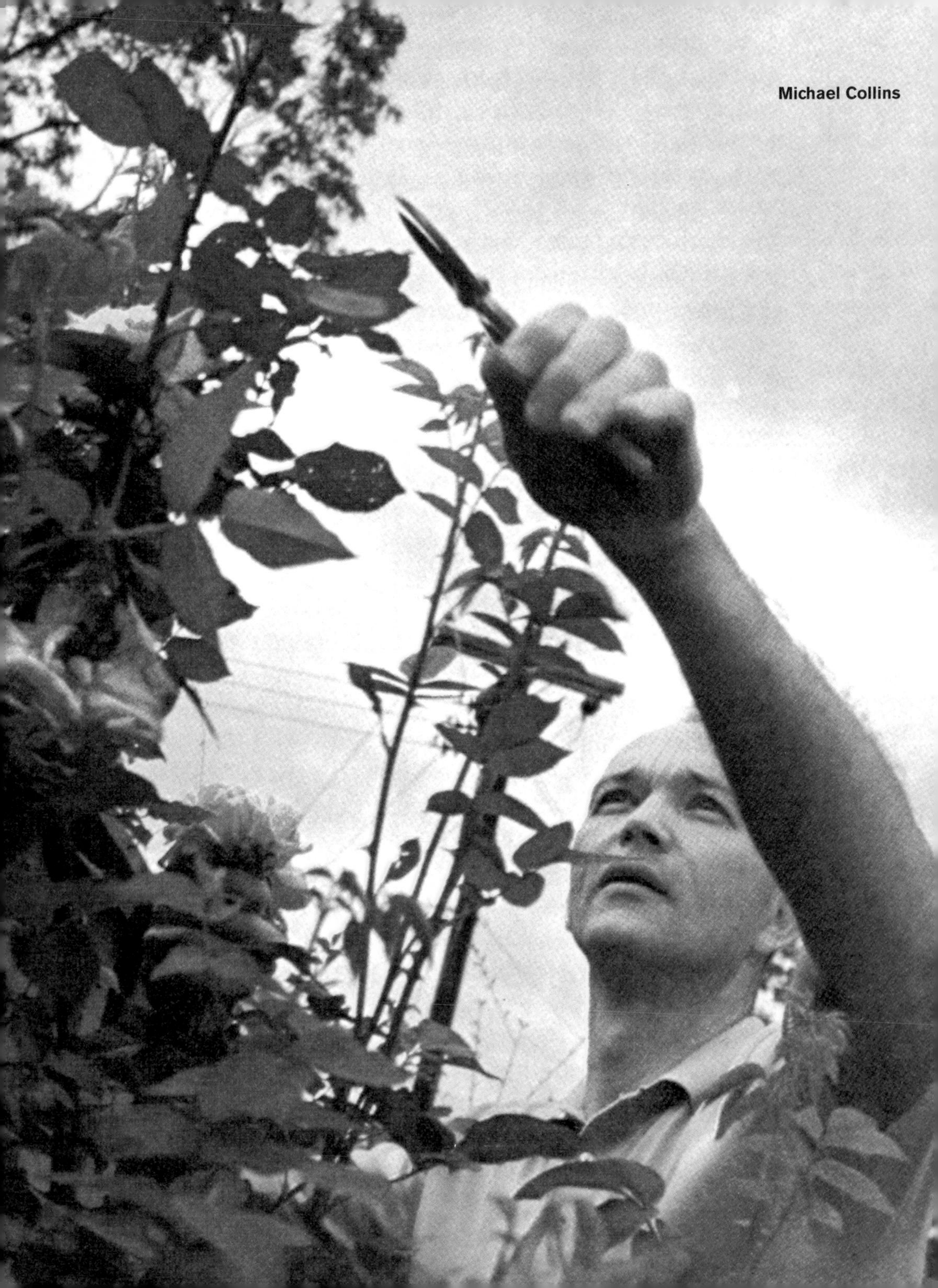
Michael Collins

Here I am,
a white male, age thirty-eight,
height 5 feet 11 inches, weight 165 pounds,
salary $ 17,000 per annum,
resident of a Texas suburb, with
black spot on my roses,
state of mind unsettled, about to
be shot off to the moon.
Yes, to the moon.

Michael Collins's notes from takeoff

ASTRONAUT

EDWIN EUGENE "BUZZ" ALDRIN

LUNAR MODULE PILOT
APOLLO 11

ASSIGNMENT:

BUZZ WILL ASSIST THE COMMANDER DURING THE MOON LANDING.

HE WILL READ ALOUD OFF ALL THE INSTRUMENTS AND REPORT ON ALTITUDE, HORIZONTAL SPEED, AND DESCENT RATE.

HE CAN ALSO PERFORM NEIL'S TASKS, JUST IN CASE.

HE WILL BE THE SECOND MAN ON THE MOON.

BACKGROUND:

WORKED AS A USAF PILOT BEFORE BEING SELECTED FOR NASA ASTRONAUT TRAINING.

3,500 HOURS OF FLYING TIME.

HAS THE HIGHEST LEVEL OF EDUCATION OF THE APOLLO 11 PILOTS. HOLDS A PH.D. IN ASTRONAUTICS. HIS THESIS WAS ON MANNED ORBITAL RENDEZVOUS—HOW TWO SPACECRAFT COULD MEET AND DOCK IN SPACE.

BORN IN MONTCLAIR, NEW JERSEY.

MISCELLANEOUS:

ATHLETIC: HE GOES FOR AN HOUR-LONG JOG EVERY MORNING.

HAS COMPETED IN POLE-VAULTING. PERSONAL BEST: 13 FEET, 9 INCHES (4.2 METERS) WITH A BAMBOO POLE.

NOT THE SOCIAL TYPE. HE'S NOT INTO SMALL TALK, BUT IF SOMEONE IS INTERESTED IN SPACE TECHNOLOGY, HE NEVER STOPS TALKING.

PERFECTIONIST.

EASY TO LIKE, BUT DIFFICULT TO GET TO KNOW.

AGE: 39 YEARS	**MARRIED TO:** JOAN (GOT MARRIED ON THEIR FIFTH DATE)	**MOTHER'S MAIDEN NAME:** MOON
BORN: JANUARY 20, 1930		**SALARY:** $18,622 PER YEAR
HEIGHT: 5 FEET, 10 INCHES (178 CENTIMETERS)	**CHILDREN:** MICHAEL, 13 JANICE, 11 ANDREW, 11	**ASTRONAUT SINCE:** 1963
WEIGHT: 165 POUNDS (75 KILOGRAMS)		**PREVIOUS SPACE TRAVEL:** GEMINI 12, 1966

NEIL ALDEN ARMSTRONG

COMMANDER
APOLLO 11

ASSIGNMENT:

NEIL IS THE COMMANDER DURING THE TRIP. ON *COLUMBIA*, HE GETS THE LAST WORD.

HE'S IN THE COMMAND SEAT DURING TAKEOFF.

HE IS ALSO THE ONE WHO WILL FLY THE LUNAR MODULE *EAGLE* AND LAND IT ON THE MOON.

BACKGROUND:

WORKED AS AN X-15 TEST PILOT BEFORE BEING SELECTED FOR NASA ASTRONAUT TRAINING.

OF ALL THE ASTRONAUTS IN THE APOLLO PROGRAM, HE IS THE MOST EXPERIENCED PILOT.

MORE THAN 4,000 HOURS OF FLYING TIME.

BORN ON A FARM IN WAPAKONETA, OHIO, A COMMUNITY WITH A POPULATION OF ONLY 7,000.

MISCELLANEOUS:

NEIL HAS ALWAYS BEEN INTERESTED IN FLYING. HE LEARNED HOW TO FLY AN AIRPLANE BEFORE HE LEARNED TO DRIVE A CAR.

HE GOT HIS PILOT'S LICENSE ON HIS 16TH BIRTHDAY.

NOT INTERESTED IN SPORTS: "I BELIEVE THAT THE GOOD LORD GAVE US A FINITE NUMBER OF HEARTBEATS AND I'M DAMNED IF I'M GOING TO USE UP MINE RUNNING UP AND DOWN A STREET."

PLAYS THE PIANO AND THE BARITONE HORN.

IS A GREAT BAKER. AS A KID HE MADE EXTRA MONEY WORKING IN A BAKERY.

AGE:
38 YEARS

MARRIED TO:
JANET
(SWIMMING INSTRUCTOR)

BORN:
AUGUST 5, 1930

SALARY:
$30,054 PER YEAR

HEIGHT:
5 FEET, 11 INCHES
(180 CENTIMETERS)

CHILDREN:
ERIC, 12
MARK, 6

ASTRONAUT SINCE:
1962

WEIGHT:
165 POUNDS
(75 KILOGRAMS)

PREVIOUS SPACE TRAVEL:
GEMINI 8, 1966

Buzz Aldrin

Neil Armstrong

The air is still at Launch Pad 39A.

At 09:31:51 the engines are ignited.

At 09:32:00 the rocket takes off from the ground.

Space is 11 minutes and 42 seconds away. That is the time it takes before Earth releases its grip on the rocket, propelling it into weightlessness.

Down on the ground, one million people are squinting at the spacecraft, now just a spot in the sky, watching it get smaller and smaller. Within moments it is lost from sight. Then it is gone altogether. People get up, fold their blankets, and head for their cars, going home or back to work. Everything is back to normal again. For everyone, except for three people.

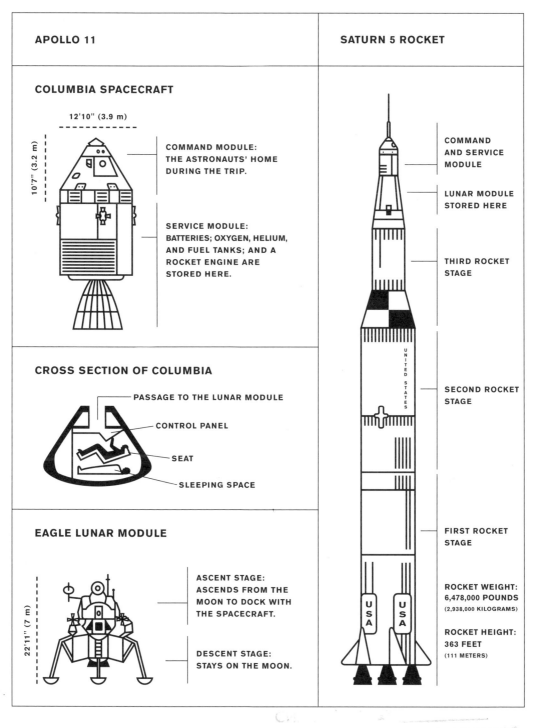

APOLLO 11

COLUMBIA SPACECRAFT

12'10" (3.9 m)

107" (3.2 m)

COMMAND MODULE:
THE ASTRONAUTS' HOME
DURING THE TRIP.

SERVICE MODULE:
BATTERIES; OXYGEN, HELIUM,
AND FUEL TANKS; AND A
ROCKET ENGINE ARE
STORED HERE.

CROSS SECTION OF COLUMBIA

PASSAGE TO THE LUNAR MODULE

CONTROL PANEL

SEAT

SLEEPING SPACE

EAGLE LUNAR MODULE

22'11" (7 m)

ASCENT STAGE:
ASCENDS FROM THE
MOON TO DOCK WITH
THE SPACECRAFT.

DESCENT STAGE:
STAYS ON THE MOON.

SATURN 5 ROCKET

COMMAND
AND SERVICE
MODULE

LUNAR MODULE
STORED HERE

THIRD ROCKET
STAGE

UNITED STATES

SECOND ROCKET
STAGE

FIRST ROCKET
STAGE

USA   USA

ROCKET WEIGHT:
6,478,000 POUNDS
(2,938,000 KILOGRAMS)

ROCKET HEIGHT:
363 FEET
(111 METERS)

WAUKESHA ELEMENTARY SCHOOLS

Many astronauts
experience space
sickness. The
weightlessness
makes them feel sick
to their stomachs
and throw up. Most
feel better after a
few days.

apollo 11,

this is **houston**

do you copy?

over.

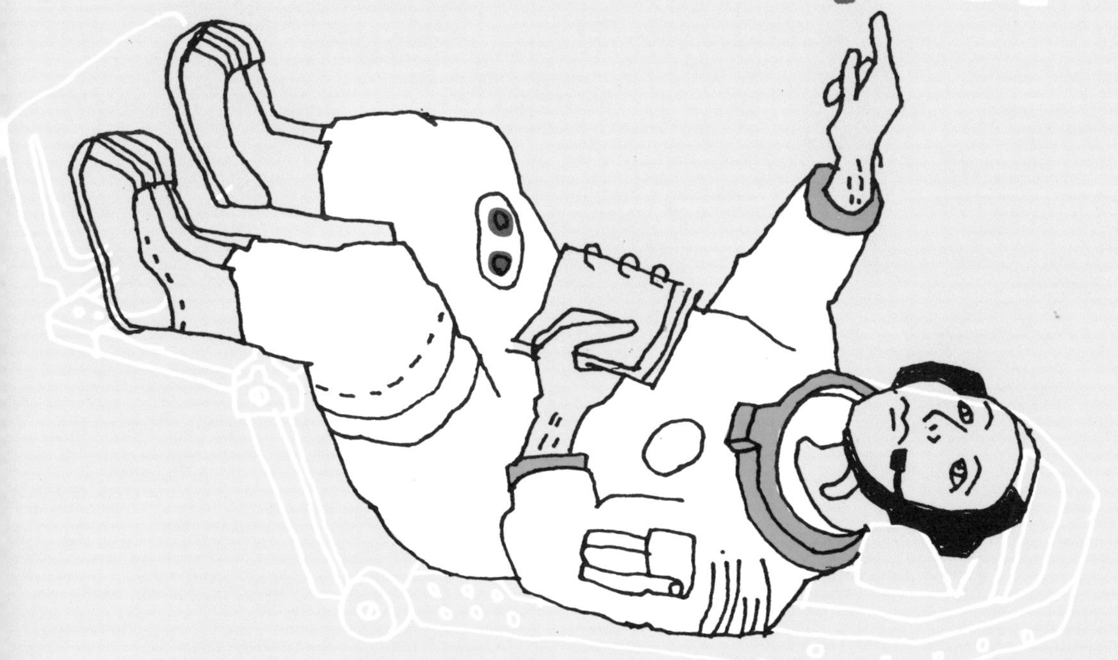

APOLLO 11 ROUND-TRIP TO THE MOON

MAXIMUM SPEED OF THE SPACECRAFT BETWEEN EARTH AND MOON: 25,000 MILES (40,000 KILOMETERS) PER HOUR
AT SPLASHDOWN IN THE OCEAN: 25 MILES (40 KILOMETERS) PER HOUR
TRAVEL TIME TO THE MOON: 3 DAYS, 4 HOURS
TRAVEL TIME FROM THE MOON: 2 DAYS, 12 HOURS (HOMEBOUND TRAVEL IS QUICKER DUE TO EARTH'S GRAVITY.)

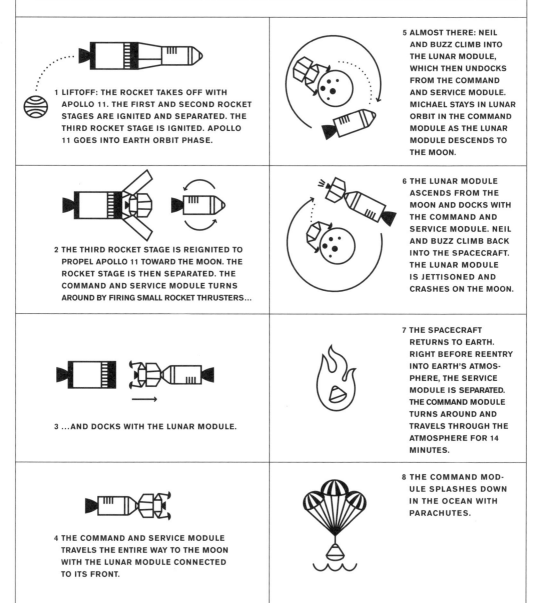

1 LIFTOFF: THE ROCKET TAKES OFF WITH APOLLO 11. THE FIRST AND SECOND ROCKET STAGES ARE IGNITED AND SEPARATED. THE THIRD ROCKET STAGE IS IGNITED. APOLLO 11 GOES INTO EARTH ORBIT PHASE.

2 THE THIRD ROCKET STAGE IS REIGNITED TO PROPEL APOLLO 11 TOWARD THE MOON. THE ROCKET STAGE IS THEN SEPARATED. THE COMMAND AND SERVICE MODULE TURNS AROUND BY FIRING SMALL ROCKET THRUSTERS...

3 ...AND DOCKS WITH THE LUNAR MODULE.

4 THE COMMAND AND SERVICE MODULE TRAVELS THE ENTIRE WAY TO THE MOON WITH THE LUNAR MODULE CONNECTED TO ITS FRONT.

5 ALMOST THERE: NEIL AND BUZZ CLIMB INTO THE LUNAR MODULE, WHICH THEN UNDOCKS FROM THE COMMAND AND SERVICE MODULE. MICHAEL STAYS IN LUNAR ORBIT IN THE COMMAND MODULE AS THE LUNAR MODULE DESCENDS TO THE MOON.

6 THE LUNAR MODULE ASCENDS FROM THE MOON AND DOCKS WITH THE COMMAND AND SERVICE MODULE. NEIL AND BUZZ CLIMB BACK INTO THE SPACECRAFT. THE LUNAR MODULE IS JETTISONED AND CRASHES ON THE MOON.

7 THE SPACECRAFT RETURNS TO EARTH. RIGHT BEFORE REENTRY INTO EARTH'S ATMOSPHERE, THE SERVICE MODULE IS SEPARATED. THE COMMAND MODULE TURNS AROUND AND TRAVELS THROUGH THE ATMOSPHERE FOR 14 MINUTES.

8 THE COMMAND MODULE SPLASHES DOWN IN THE OCEAN WITH PARACHUTES.

The interior of the spacecraft *Columbia* is as small as the inside of an ordinary car. The capsule is the astronauts' living room, office, kitchen, bedroom, and bathroom. It is equipped with 15 miles (24 kilometers) of power cables. It is made of two million pieces. This means that even if 99.9 percent of all the components were working, there would still be 2,000 broken pieces.

Despite the fact that the capsule is so small, it is easy to lose things due to weightlessness. Since everything floats away as soon as it is put down, the astronauts have attached hundreds of Velcro pieces to the walls of the capsule to hold lists, pens, sunglasses, star maps, and packs of gum.

Michael, Buzz, and Neil know their capsule inside out. They have spent more than half a year inside it, down on Earth, preparing for this trip. Glued everywhere on the control panels are tiny pieces of plastic where the astronauts have jotted down notes to themselves in their neatest handwriting:

BOIL>50

S-BAND AUX TO TAPE

90 SEC PRIOR TO DUMP

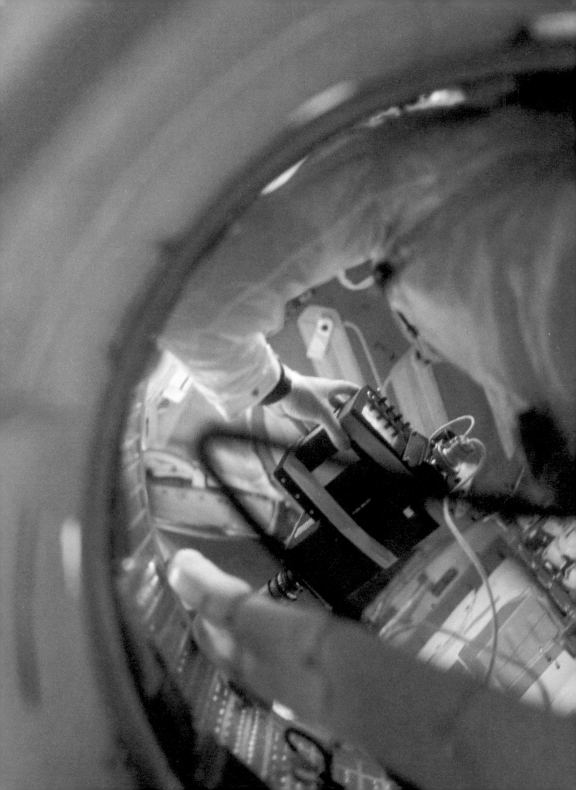

The astronauts don't do anything without first looking it up on their checklists. They call the lists the "fourth passenger." The lists describe *what* they should do and *when* they should do it. Page after page of instructions must be followed in the correct order: the astronauts must control the pressure in the cabin; read the fuel, hydrogen, and oxygen meters; and report to planet Earth. They must vacuum the air to prevent crumbs from sneaking into the electric system. Once every 24 hours they must empty their urine-collecting devices through a vent in the capsule wall. (As soon as the urine molecules are scattered into space, they freeze to ice and are transformed into a sparkling cloud.) The checklists are the result of years of training in the simulators down on Earth. Each astronaut has his own set of checklists. Together, Michael, Buzz, and Neil have brought with them 20 pounds (9 kilograms) of lists.

Michael Collins makes notes on his checklists to help future Apollo astronauts. During liftoff, the astronauts realized that a thigh pocket on Neil's space suit was just about to be snagged on the abort handle. Had the handle been turned just a little bit to the left, the capsule would have been ejected and splashed down in the ocean.

Repeat above steps with buffer ampoule
POT H2O IN vlv - OPEN (verify)
Wait 10 min & remove ampoule of H2O
Replace chlor port cap
Stow chlorination unit
Do not drink for 30 min

21 WASTE WATER TANK DRAIN
H2O QTY IND sw - WASTE
POTABLE TANK INLET - CLOSE
WATER CONT PRESS REL vlv - DUMP A
Monitor H2O QTY (WASTE) ind - decreasing
When H2O QTY (WASTE) ind reads 25%:
  WATER CONT PRESS REL vlv - 2
POTABLE TANK INLET - OPEN

22 SIDE HATCH URINE/WATER DUMP
Remove Dump Nozzle Conn Cover
Remove Plug & Stow
Withdraw Wire Guard & Wires from slot
Install Male QD on Dump Nozzle
Connect cable to heater connector (crew option)
     UTIL PWR - OFF
     Connect cable to utility outlet
     UTIL PWR - ON
Connect Urine Dump Hose to Dump Nozzle QD
Connect other end of UT hose to UTS/
  Waste Servicing Tank (as req)
Dump Waste Water/Urine
Disconnect UT hose from UTS/Waste Servicing Tank
  and Purge
Disconnect UT Hose from Dump Nozzle & stow
UTIL PWR - OFF (verify)
Disconnect Cable from heater & outlet
     & stow (verify)
Install plug & dump nozzle connector

23 WATER COLLECTION
Connect urine transfer hose-filter to urine/feces QD
Connect cabin purge QD to urine transfer hose
WASTE MANAGEMENT DRAIN vlv - DUMP
Collect water

CS 107 & SUBS

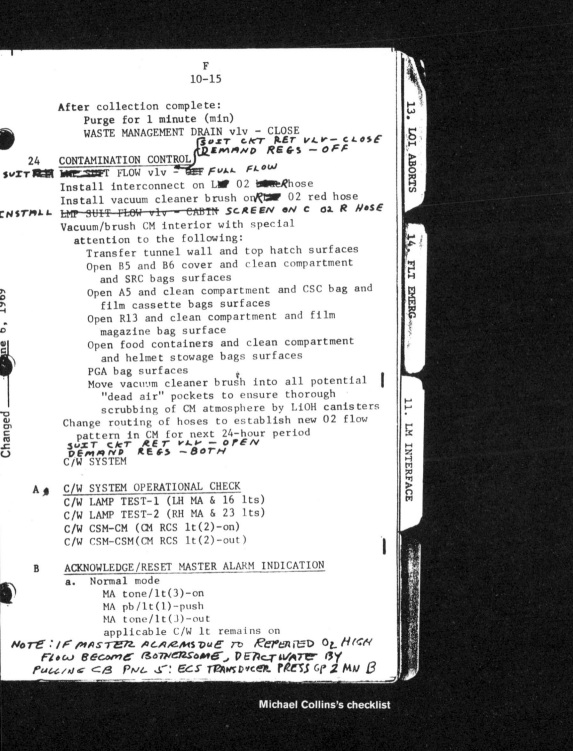

After collection complete:
    Purge for 1 minute (min)
    WASTE MANAGEMENT DRAIN vlv – CLOSE
    {SUIT CKT RET VLV - CLOSE
    {DEMAND REGS - OFF

24 CONTAMINATION CONTROL
SUIT RET ~~LMP SUIT~~ FLOW vlv – ~~GET~~ *FULL FLOW*
Install interconnect on L~~MP~~ 02 ~~blue~~Rhose
Install vacuum cleaner brush on ~~RH~~ 02 red hose
INSTALL ~~LMP SUIT FLOW vlv - CABIN~~ *SCREEN ON C 02 R HOSE*
Vacuum/brush CM interior with special
  attention to the following:
    Transfer tunnel wall and top hatch surfaces
    Open B5 and B6 cover and clean compartment
      and SRC bags surfaces
    Open A5 and clean compartment and CSC bag and
      film cassette bags surfaces
    Open R13 and clean compartment and film
      magazine bag surface
    Open food containers and clean compartment
      and helmet stowage bags surfaces
    PGA bag surfaces
    Move vacuum cleaner brush into all potential |
      "dead air" pockets to ensure thorough
      scrubbing of CM atmosphere by LiOH canisters
Change routing of hoses to establish new 02 flow
  pattern in CM for next 24-hour period
SUIT CKT RET VLV - OPEN
DEMAND REGS - BOTH
C/W SYSTEM

A C/W SYSTEM OPERATIONAL CHECK
C/W LAMP TEST-1 (LH MA & 16 lts)
C/W LAMP TEST-2 (RH MA & 23 lts)
C/W CSM-CM (CM RCS lt(2)-on)
C/W CSM-CSM(CM RCS lt(2)-out) |

B ACKNOWLEDGE/RESET MASTER ALARM INDICATION
a. Normal mode
    MA tone/lt(3)-on
    MA pb/lt(1)-push
    MA tone/lt(3)-out
    applicable C/W lt remains on
NOTE: IF MASTER ALARMS DUE TO REPEATED O₂ HIGH
FLOW BECOME BOTHERSOME, DEACTIVATE BY
PULLING CB PNL 5: ECS TRANSDUCER PRESS GP 2 MN B

Left margin (vertical):
Changed ____ ~~ne~~ 6, 1969

Right margin tabs:
13. LOI ABORTS
14. FLT EMERG
11. LM INTERFACE

Michael Collins's checklist

In space, astronauts'
spines straighten due
to weightlessness
and they become one
to two inches taller.
Their waists narrow
as their internal
organs move upward.
And their faces look
puffy since the blood
that is supposed to
be in their legs ends
up in their heads.

Michael Collins inside *Columbia*

PERSONAL BELONGINGS

SINCE THE CAPSULE IS SO SMALL AND IT IS IMPORTANT THAT THE LUGGAGE WEIGH AS LITTLE AS POSSIBLE, THE ASTRONAUTS MUST BE ABLE TO FIT THEIR PERSONAL THINGS IN A PERSONAL PREFERENCE KIT, A PPK. IT IS A SMALL BAG MADE FROM WHITE FIBERGLASS CLOTH, MEASURING 2 x 4 x 8 INCHES (5 x 10 x 20 CENTIMETERS).

MICHAEL BRINGS:

POEMS AND PRAYERS

OBJECTS THAT WILL MAKE GREAT GIFTS ONCE HE RETURNS:
  COINS
  CUFF LINKS
  TIE PINS
  LITTLE FLAGS
  CRUCIFIXES
  MEDALLIONS
  INSIGNIA
  RINGS

A SMALL, HOLLOW LUCKY BEAN CHARM FROM INDIA (INSIDE THE BEAN, THERE ARE 50 TINY CARVED IVORY ELEPHANTS.)

1 PPK FOR THE COMMAND MODULE

BUZZ BRINGS:

HIS MOTHER'S LUCKY CHARM BRACELET, ENGRAVED WITH THE NAMES OF HER CHILDREN AND GRANDCHILDREN

FOUR GOLD OLIVE BRANCHES, ONE THAT HE WILL LEAVE ON THE MOON AND ONE FOR EACH OF THE ASTRONAUTS' WIVES

A SMALL VIAL OF WINE, A TINY CHALICE, AND A WAFER (BUZZ INTENDS TO TAKE HOLY COMMUNION ONCE THEY HAVE LANDED ON THE MOON.)

1 PPK FOR THE COMMAND MODULE

1 PPK FOR THE LUNAR MODULE

NEIL BRINGS:

AN AUDIOTAPE FOR THE *COLUMBIA* CASSETTE PLAYER, WITH MUSIC RECORDED BY HIS WIFE, JANET

A SMALL PIECE OF THE PROPELLER FROM *KITTY HAWK*, THE FIRST POWERED AIRCRAFT, FROM 1903

(NEIL ALSO SMUGGLES MINT LIFESAVERS AND A COMB IN THE POCKET OF HIS SPACE SUIT.)

1 PPK FOR THE COMMAND MODULE

1 PPK FOR THE LUNAR MODULE

TOGETHER THE ASTRONAUTS BRING:

15 PACKS OF CHEWING GUM

AUDIOTAPES WITH SONGS THAT HAVE THE WORD "MOON" IN THE LYRICS AND WITH TAPED SOUNDS FROM EARTH: JUNGLE NOISES, TRAINS, DOGS BARKING

There is no night in space. When Michael, Buzz, and Neil go to bed the first night, they have to cover the windows because the sun is so bright. When they have finished brushing their teeth, they must swallow the toothpaste foam since there is no place to spit it out. The astronauts fasten themselves into thin white sleeping bags so that they won't float around the capsule while they sleep. They lie there, in the faint yellow light from the control panel, listening to the sounds of the capsule: the muffled noise from the air conditioning, the snapping sounds from the batteries. They have been awake for more than 18 hours, but the astronauts still can't sleep. They travel farther and farther away from planet Earth.

Astronauts sleep less in space. Their snoring is louder because their faces are full of fluid. Weightlessness makes their heads nod back and forth as their pulse beats in their necks. And the cabin pressure is so low that it creates an unpleasant sensation in their mouths called "cotton fuzz."

38

apollo 11, this
is houston, we're
three minutes away
from loss of signal

over

CLOTHES

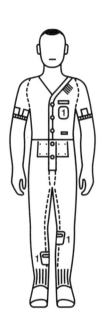

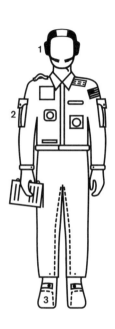

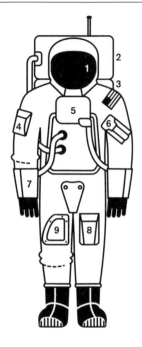

UNDERGARMENT

THE ASTRONAUTS WEAR THEIR
ONE-PIECE UNDERGARMENT
DURING THE ENTIRE TRIP, EVEN
WHEN THEY SLEEP.

1 RADIATION METER

IN-FLIGHT COVERALLS

1 SNOOPY CAP WITH EAR-
  PHONES AND MICROPHONE
  FOR RADIO COMMUNICATION
  WITH EARTH
2 POCKETS FOR LITTLE OBJECTS
3 SOFT SLIPPERS WITH VELCRO
  ON THE BOTTOMS (SO THAT
  THE ASTRONAUTS CAN ATTACH
  THEMSELVES TO THE FLOOR,
  WALLS, OR CEILING OF THE
  CAPSULE)

SPACE SUIT

1 VISOR PROTECTING AGAINST
  UV AND INFRARED RAYS ON
  THE MOON
2 EMERGENCY OXYGEN SUPPLY
  (LASTS FOR 30 MINUTES)
3 REGULAR OXYGEN SUPPLY
  (LASTS FOR FOUR HOURS), BAT-
  TERIES, COOLING SYSTEM,
  RADIO
4 POCKET FOR SUNGLASSES
5 REMOTE-CONTROL PANEL FOR
  COOLING SYSTEM AND OTHER
  SUIT FEATURES
6 POCKET FOR FLASHLIGHT
7 CHECKLISTS
8 POCKET FOR VARIOUS OBJECTS,
  LIKE MOON SAMPLES
9 URINE CONTAINER

During the day, the astronauts wear their one-piece under-garment and in-flight coveralls in the spacecraft. They only wear the space suit during launch, while docking, in the lunar module, and on the moon. Despite the fact that they are tailormade for each astronaut, the suits are uncomfortable, especially around the shoulders. Michael Collins hates wearing his space suit. It makes him claustrophobic. It's difficult to breathe in the suit—he feels that he's not getting enough air. Many times he has considered quitting his job as an astronaut just because he hates being trapped inside the space suit.

Inside the space suit it is so quiet that the sounds the body makes can be heard: breathing in and out, blood pulsating in the ears, even muscles flexing in the arms and legs. Under their space suits, the astronauts wear diapers and overalls covered with 266 feet (81 meters) of thin tubes filled with cold water, which prevents the astronauts from overheating. The suit is made with 22 layers that must protect against the vacuum of space and insulate against the tem-perature variations on the moon: -250°F (-180°C) at night and +250°F (+120°C) in the day.

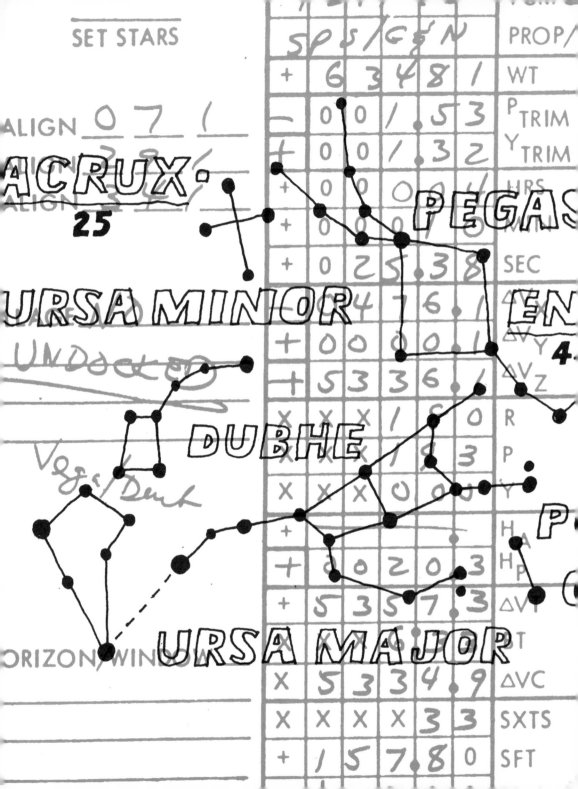

Houston, Apollo 11...
I've got the world in my window.

Michael Collins, 28 hours, 7 minutes after liftoff

The air in the capsule, pure oxygen, smells different from ordinary air: at first it is ice cold and smells like a hospital. When the astronauts have gone to the "bathroom"—a small plastic bag—the smell lingers in weightlessness. So does the smell of their sweat. After a few days, the entire capsule smells pretty bad.

Michael Collins uses the stars to navigate. The spacecraft's computer requires the position of 37 specific stars to calculate *Columbia*'s exact location. If the craft goes off course, Michael must ignite small steering rockets to get it back on the right track. Although the spacecraft is traveling at a speed varying from 2,000 to 25,000 miles (3,200 to 40,000 kilometers) per hour, the astronauts can't feel it. But every time they look out the windows, they can see that Earth has shrunk and the moon has grown bigger and bigger.

It was a totally different moon than I had ever seen before. The moon that I knew from old was a yellow flat disk, and this was a huge three-dimensional sphere, almost a ghostly blue-tinged sort of pale white.

It didn't seem like a very friendly or welcoming place. It made one wonder whether we should be invading its domain or not.

Michael Collins

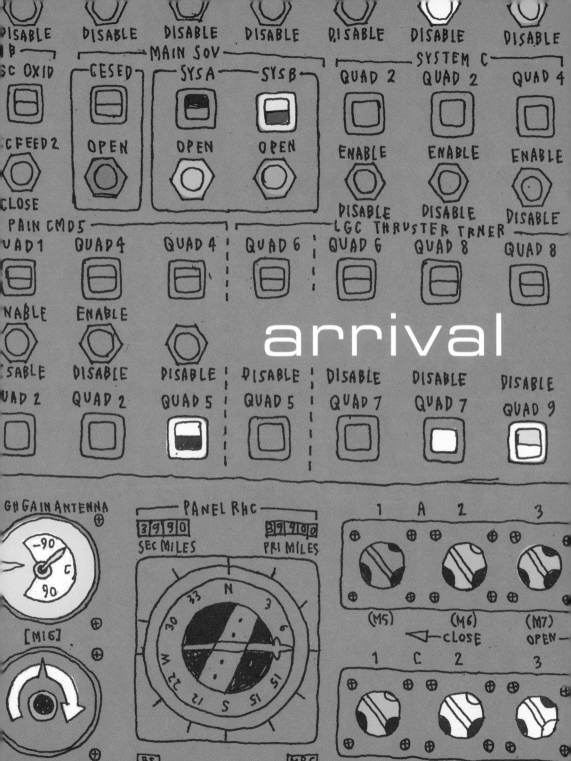

It is July 20, 1969. A Sunday. It's four minutes to ten in the morning. It is -250°F (-180°C) in the shade and +250°F (+120°C) in the sun at the Sea of Tranquility, where Neil and Buzz have landed the *Eagle*. They are 242,000 miles (390,000 kilometers) from Launch Pad 39A at Kennedy Space Center in Florida.

In the earliest versions of the checklists, Buzz Aldrin would be the first man to step down onto the moon. But the lunar module hatch opens inward to the right, and Buzz, who stood right behind it, had difficulty climbing out. When the astronauts tried to switch places during practice, they damaged the cramped cabin. A few months before the launch, it was decided that Neil should go first. He crawls backward through a tiny hatch near the floor. As he looks toward the horizon, he can see that they have landed on a sphere: the horizon is a little bent since the moon is so small. His arms are covered with goose bumps. There is no air. No sound. No life. No footprints.

Wait: now there is one.

Neil Armstrong is the first man on the moon.

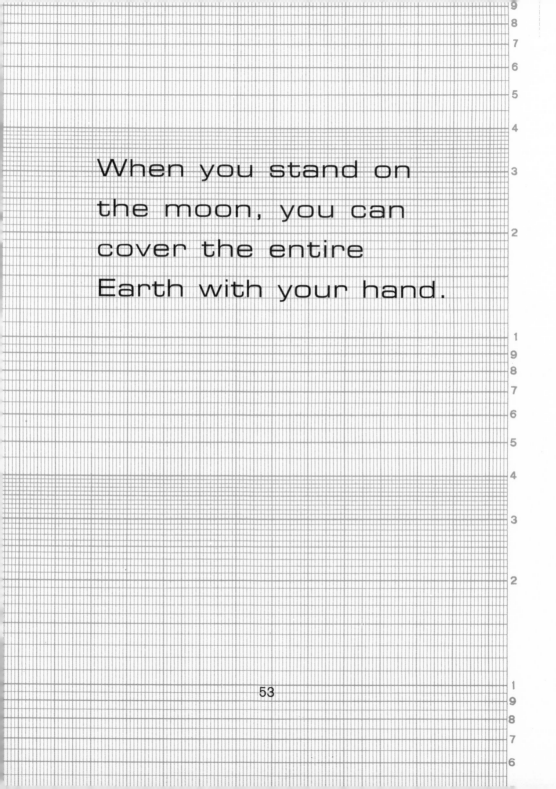

When you stand on
the moon, you can
cover the entire
Earth with your hand.

242,000 miles (390,000 kilometers) from home, trapped inside a small vessel, two men are taking snapshots of each other.

Buzz Aldrin's picture of Neil Armstrong

Neil Armstrong's picture of Buzz Aldrin

In case something unexpected should happen,
the astronauts never bounce farther than 200 feet
(60 meters) from the landing site.

OK. We copy you down, Eagle

Neil and Buzz stay on the moon for 21 hours and 36 minutes, but only a little more than 2 hours of that time is spent outside the lunar module. They perform three minor experiments and load two aluminum suitcases with 48 pounds (22 kilograms) of moon dust and rocks.

The three minor experiments:

    To measure solar particles

    To measure the exact distance to Earth

    To measure moonquakes and meteoritic impact

The major experiment:

    To land on the moon

When they have climbed back into the lunar module and shut the hatch, they take their helmets off. They look at each other because they both sense a strong smell. Neil thinks it smells like wet ashes. Buzz says it smells like spent gunpowder. It is the moon. The moon has a smell.

on the far side

BACTERIAL
FILTER STOWAGE

(F6)   (F8)   (G3)   (G6)   (G8)

AUDIO CTR NORM   SUIT POWER NORM   INTERCOM VOLUME   OFF   VHF AM VOLUME   S-BAND

5

OFF   OFF   OFF   OFF

(S6)   (S8)   (R3)   (R6)   (R8)

of the moon

ROLL
350

PITCH
350

YAW
350

RCV   OFF   1 T/R   1 PTT   AUDIO

2   2

(S8)   (S7)   (S6)   (S5)   (S4)

FC 3

INV 3
TEMP HI

SM RCS
D

PITCH
GMBL 1

PITCH

PAD COMM   VOX   MASTER VOLUME   VOX SENS   AUDIO/TONE

MODE
INTERCOM
/PTT

(S1)   (R1)   (R2)   (S2)

0   1   2   3   4

RCV   RCV   RCV   RCV

Six hundred million people in 47 countries are watching the blurred TV transmission of the lunar landing. There is one person who has no chance of catching Neil and Buzz on TV. He is traveling at a height of 70 miles (110 kilometers) above the far side of the moon. All he can see is darkness and stars outside his window.

Michael Collins has 28 hours to go, alone in the capsule. He has trained for so long. He has traveled so far. He is so close now and still he can't land on the moon. They did not choose him.

He was going for 99 percent of the trip and that was good enough for him, he has replied when people have asked. But he knew he didn't have the best seat on *Columbia*.

He thinks to himself that he never really got to know the astronauts who are now on the moon. Neil and Buzz trained together for many months in the lunar module simulator. Michael trained by himself in the capsule.

do looks simple
not so-launch vehicle
es must light urine
or stranded particle
ad like angels
ave confidence

From Michael Collins's notepad in *Columbia*

Once every two hours *Columbia* passes over the landing
site. Michael Collins tries to locate the *Eagle*. He can't see
it. He only sees crater after crater, cast with sharp shadows
from the sun.

On the backside of the moon,
on the night side, you can't
see the surface. The moon is defined
simply by the absence of stars.

The laws of physics tell you
that your fine spacecraft is in
an orbit sixty miles above it and
there's no way you can hit
anything. But the thought
        does occur,

        Gosh,
I'm skimming along just barely over
the surface of a strange planet.

Michael Collins

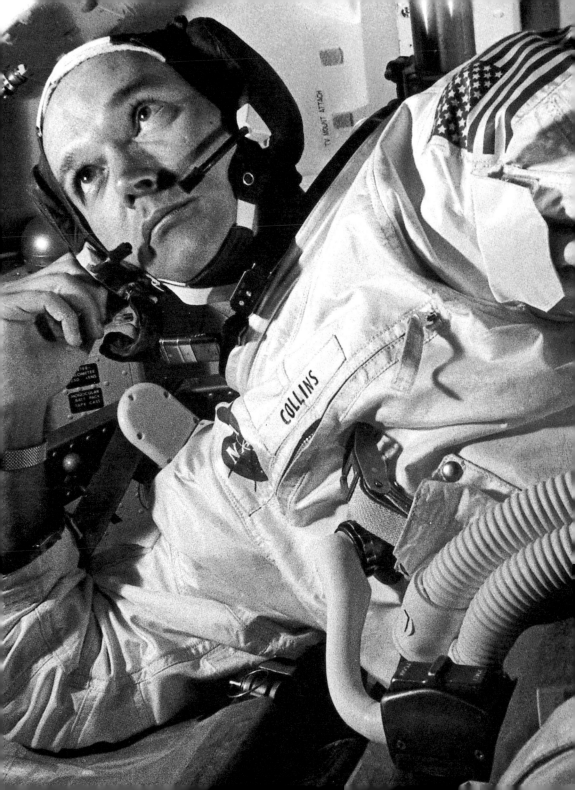

Every other hour, all radio communication with Earth is lost as the spacecraft skims over the far side of the moon. When Neil and Buzz are on the moon's surface, Michael Collins has to do three people's jobs. He has to make 850 computer commands. He has been taught just *how* to push the buttons—hard, right in the center, and to hold them pushed for a little over a second. They must be pushed in the right order, one after the other: VERB—88—ENTER. VERB—87—ENTER. If he loses track on the far side of the moon, there is no one to ask.

Michael turns up the light in the command module. It's almost cozy. He is used to flying alone. He has flown airplanes by himself for almost 20 years. He has even practiced how he should return home by himself if something should happen to Neil and Buzz down on the moon.

It's quiet in the capsule on the dark side of the moon. The only noises are the fans humming and a faint crackling from the radio. Michael Collins prepares his dinner. Looks out the windows. Every 120th minute he sees the Earth rise at the horizon.

MICHAEL COLLINS'S FOOD PACK ON THE FOURTH DAY OF THE TRIP

BREAKFAST:

FROSTED FLAKES
(FREEZE-DRIED)

4 PEANUT CUBES
(BITE-SIZED)

COCOA (POWDER)

ORANGE AND GRAPEFRUIT
DRINK (POWDER)

CANADIAN BACON AND
APPLESAUCE (FREEZE-
DRIED)

LUNCH:

SHRIMP COCKTAIL
(FREEZE-DRIED)

HAM AND POTATOES
(WET-PACK)

FRUIT COCKTAIL
(FREEZE-DRIED)

4 DATE FRUITCAKE CUBES
(BITE-SIZED)

GRAPEFRUIT DRINK
(POWDER)

DINNER:

BEEF STEW (SPOON-BOWL)

4 COCONUT CUBES
(BITE-SIZED)

BANANA PUDDING (POWDER)

GRAPE PUNCH (POWDER)

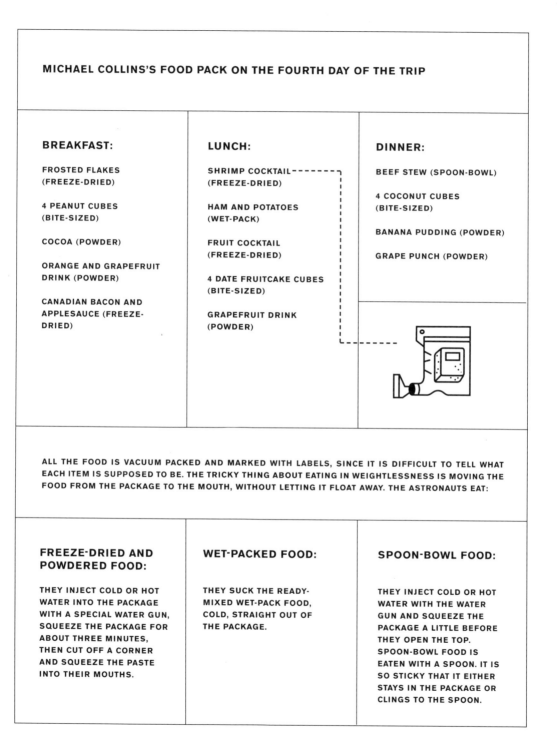

ALL THE FOOD IS VACUUM PACKED AND MARKED WITH LABELS, SINCE IT IS DIFFICULT TO TELL WHAT
EACH ITEM IS SUPPOSED TO BE. THE TRICKY THING ABOUT EATING IN WEIGHTLESSNESS IS MOVING THE
FOOD FROM THE PACKAGE TO THE MOUTH, WITHOUT LETTING IT FLOAT AWAY. THE ASTRONAUTS EAT:

FREEZE-DRIED AND POWDERED FOOD:

THEY INJECT COLD OR HOT
WATER INTO THE PACKAGE
WITH A SPECIAL WATER GUN,
SQUEEZE THE PACKAGE FOR
ABOUT THREE MINUTES,
THEN CUT OFF A CORNER
AND SQUEEZE THE PASTE
INTO THEIR MOUTHS.

WET-PACKED FOOD:

THEY SUCK THE READY-
MIXED WET-PACK FOOD,
COLD, STRAIGHT OUT OF
THE PACKAGE.

SPOON-BOWL FOOD:

THEY INJECT COLD OR HOT
WATER WITH THE WATER
GUN AND SQUEEZE THE
PACKAGE A LITTLE BEFORE
THEY OPEN THE TOP.
SPOON-BOWL FOOD IS
EATEN WITH A SPOON. IT IS
SO STICKY THAT IT EITHER
STAYS IN THE PACKAGE OR
CLINGS TO THE SPOON.

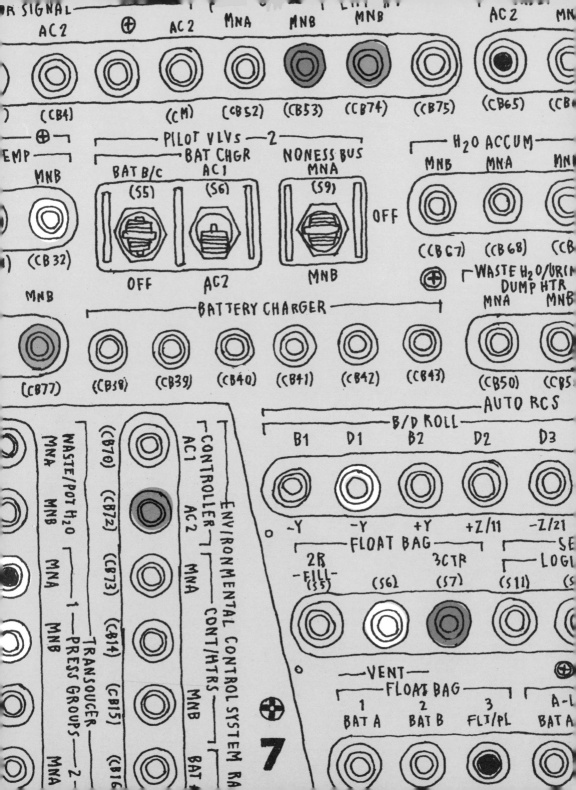

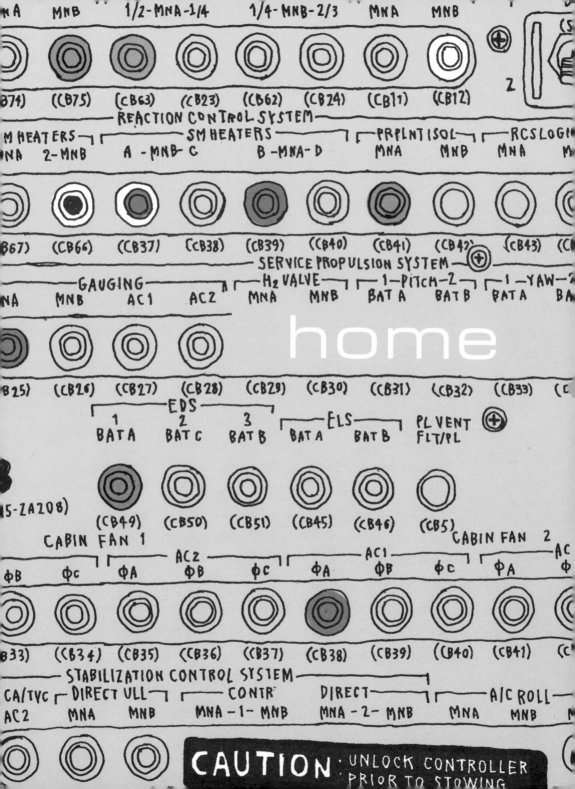

home

It is July 24, 1969. A Thursday. Ever since they left the moon, the astronauts have been eager to get back home. After 8 days, 3 hours, and 18 minutes in *Columbia* without washing, the entire body itches. It is hard to breathe in the spacecraft now. It smells like wet dogs and rotten swamp. Michael Collins has flown *Columbia* during reentry into the Earth's atmosphere. For 14 minutes, the astronauts have been pushed down into their seats. They have weighed seven times their weight on Earth. Now the capsule has splashed down in the ocean near Hawaii.

No one knows if the astronauts have been exposed to dangerous lunar germs that could potentially wipe out the human race. Because of this they are sent straight to a quarantine facility: a silver-colored mobile home. Inside, the astronauts write reports about their trip. Michael beats Neil in cards. As they sit there, bored as can be, they begin to understand just what they have experienced. During the trip itself they were so focused on their job that they didn't have time to think about what they have actually done. Everyone on Earth gathered together because of the moon landing. But the astronauts themselves have been far, far away.

As they watch a taped recording of the moon landing, Buzz suddenly turns to Neil and says: "Neil, we missed the whole thing!"

In the past, Michael Collins never really cared about the machines he has flown, but this time it's different. On the second night of quarantine, he climbs back into *Columbia* and takes a seat. Then he leans over and scribbles a message in ballpoint pen on the capsule wall, in the tiniest handwriting imaginable:

Spacecraft 107–alias Apollo 11–alias Columbia
The best ship to come down the line
God bless her
Michael Collins, CMP

To find out if the astronauts are carrying deadly germs, mice are let into the quarantine trailer. The mice have grown up in a germ-free laboratory. After 17 days the astronauts are let out. For the first time in a month they breathe fresh air. If the mice had died, Michael Collins, Buzz Aldrin, and Neil Armstrong might still be quarantined.

LEFT ON THE MOON

SINCE APOLLO 11, THERE HAVE BEEN FIVE OTHER LUNAR MODULES ON THE MOON. THE LAST ONE LANDED IN 1972. EVERYTHING THE ASTRONAUTS LEFT BEHIND STAYS EXACTLY LIKE IT WAS WHEN IT WAS FIRST PUT THERE. THERE IS NO RUST. THERE IS NO WEAR AND TEAR. IN THE GRAY MOON DUST LIE THE TRACES OF SIX APOLLO MISSIONS:

2 GOLF BALLS HIT BY ASTRONAUT ALAN SHEPARD (APOLLO 14)

TO SAVE ON WEIGHT, THE ASTRONAUTS LEFT EVERY-THING THEY DIDN'T NEED BEFORE TAKING OFF IN THE LUNAR MODULE:
  SCIENTIFIC EXPERIMENTS
  TV CAMERAS AND CABLES
  HASSELBLAD CAMERAS
  EMPTY FOOD PACKAGES

PARTS OF THE SPACE SUITS:
  BACKPACKS
  BOOTS
  URINE CONTAINERS

6 LUNAR MODULES

3 MOON BUGGIES (FROM APOLLO 15, 16, AND 17)

MEMENTOS AND HONORARY OBJECTS:
  PLAQUES
  MEDALLIONS
  ASTRONAUT BADGES
  CRUCIFIXES
  A GOLD OLIVE BRANCH
  A COMPUTER DISC THE SIZE OF A SILVER DOLLAR WITH PEACEFUL GREETINGS FROM PRESIDENTS AND PRIME MINISTERS OF 73 COUNTRIES

A SCULPTURE OF A FALLEN ASTRONAUT, IN MEMORY OF ALL THOSE WHO HAVE DIED IN THE EFFORTS TO REACH THE MOON

ONE RED BIBLE

6 AMERICAN FLAGS

UNVERIFIED:
  LAS BRISAS HOTEL IN ACAPULCO, MEXICO, INSISTS THAT THE APOLLO 11 ASTRONAUTS PLACED A PINK FLAG FROM THE HOTEL ON THE MOON IN GRATITUDE FOR THEIR COMPLIMENTARY STAY.

OVER FOUR HUNDRED SIXTY THOUSAND PEOPLE WORKED ON THE APOLLO PROJECT. THEY GOT 12 ASTRONAUTS TO THE MOON. ALTOGETHER, THE APOLLO ASTRONAUTS BROUGHT 840 POUNDS (380 KILOGRAMS) OF MOON MATERIAL BACK TO EARTH. ON THE MOON THERE ARE FOOTPRINTS FROM 12 PEOPLE, TRACES THAT WILL NEVER BE SWEPT AWAY BY ANY WIND.

This picture of Apollo 16 astronaut Charlie Duke and his family, Dottie, Charles Jr., and Thomas, has been lying in the exact same place on the moon since 1972.

MICHAEL COLLINS

DECLINED THE OFFER TO BECOME COMMANDER OF APOLLO 17. IF HE HAD ACCEPTED, HE WOULD HAVE BEEN THE LAST MAN ON THE MOON. MICHAEL COLLINS QUIT BEING AN ASTRONAUT AND BECAME THE DIRECTOR OF THE NATIONAL AIR AND SPACE MUSEUM IN WASHINGTON, D.C. HE IS NOW RETIRED AND LIKES TO SPEND HIS TIME FISHING.

BUZZ ALDRIN

WAS NEVER QUITE SATISFIED WITH BEING THE SECOND MAN ON THE MOON, INSTEAD OF THE FIRST. FOR A TIME, HE SUFFERED FROM DEPRESSION, AND WAS HOSPITALIZED. THESE DAYS, BUZZ RUNS A COMPANY THAT DEVELOPS SPACE PROJECTS.

NEIL ARMSTRONG

WAS NEVER INTERESTED IN BECOMING A SUPERSTAR. HE BOUGHT A DAIRY. FOR EIGHT YEARS HE WORKED AS A UNIVERSITY PROFESSOR, TEACHING AEROSPACE ENGINEERING. NOW NEIL IS RETIRED. HE RARELY GIVES INTERVIEWS.

When Michael Collins returned from the moon, he made a decision to never travel again. He wanted to spend the rest of his life fishing, bringing up his children, taking care of his dogs, and sitting on the porch with his wife.

Sometimes, when he's talking to other people, the thought strikes him: I have been to places and done things that no one can ever imagine. I will never be able to explain what it was like. I carry it inside, like a treasure.

At night, Michael Collins tends to the roses in his garden at the back of his house. The soil smells good. The wind feels warm and humid against his face. He looks up at the yellow disk in the sky and thinks to himself: I have been there. It was beautiful, but compared to Earth it was nothing.

He never wants to go back to the moon.

We're lucky to have
this planet. I know.

Michael Collins

APOLLO

Name of the U.S. space program during the years 1967–75. The spacecraft were made for three people. Manned moon missions:

Apollo 1: 1967. Astronauts Grissom, White, and Chaffee were killed in a fire in the command module during a pre-flight test on the ground.

Apollo 7: 1968. Astronauts Schirra, Eisele, Cunningham.

Apollo 8: 1968. Astronauts Borman, Lovell, Anders.

Apollo 9: 1969. Astronauts McDivitt, Scott, Schweickart.

Apollo 10: 1969. Astronauts Stafford, Young, Cernan.

Apollo 11: 1969. Astronauts Armstrong, Collins, Aldrin. First moon landing.

Apollo 12: 1969. Astronauts Conrad, Gordon, Bean. Second moon landing.

Apollo 13: 1970. Astronauts Lovell, Swigert, Haise. On the way to the moon, a tank of liquid oxygen exploded in the service module. The moon landing had to be canceled; the astronauts moved into the lunar module in order to survive and made a dramatic return to Earth.

Apollo 14: 1971. Astronauts Shepard, Roosa, Mitchell. Third moon landing.

Apollo 15: 1971. Astronauts Scott, Worden, Irwin. Fourth moon landing.

Apollo 16: 1972. Astronauts Young, Mattingly, Duke. Fifth moon landing.

Apollo 17: 1972. Astronauts Cernan, Evans, Schmitt. Sixth moon landing, the last so far.

ASTRONAUT

From Greek *aster,* "star," and *nautes,* "sailor." Space traveler. Russian space travelers are called *cosmonauts.*

COLUMBIA

The command module, the capsule of Apollo 11.

COMMANDER

The captain of the space trip.

COMMAND MODULE

Where the astronauts stayed during their trip. The only part of the Apollo 11 spacecraft that returned to Earth.

COSMONAUT

From the Greek *kosmos,* "universe," and *nautes,* "sailor." Russian term for astronaut.

CRATER

Hole in the lunar surface. Most lunar craters are created by meteoric impact.

CSM PILOT

The astronaut who navigates the spacecraft to and from the moon. He stays in the command module as the commander and lunar module pilot land on the moon with the lunar module.

DOCK

The last step in a space rendezvous, when two spacecraft connect.

EAGLE

Lunar module, Apollo 11.

GEMINI

Name of the U.S. space program during the years 1965–66 for manned space flights (docking, space rendezvous, and space walks). The spacecraft were made for two people. Gemini was an intermediate program between Mercury (one astronaut) and Apollo (three astronauts).

GRAVITY

Gravitational pull. On Earth: 1 g. The moon has one-sixth of Earth's gravity: $1/6$ g (0.17 x Earth's gravity).

HOUSTON

NASA's center for manned space flight. It housed Mission Control–the people who carried out radio communication with the Apollo astronauts.

KENNEDY SPACE CENTER (KSC)

NASA's center for rocket launches in Florida. All the Apollo missions took off from KSC.

LUNAR MODULE

Two-part spacecraft brought along by Apollo 5 and Apollo 9 through 17. Its only function is to descend to and ascend from the moon.

LUNAR MODULE PILOT

Commander's copilot during the moon landing.

MOON

Earth's natural satellite. Diameter: 2,160 miles (3,476 kilometers). The distance to the moon varies, but is on average 238,900 miles (384,400 kilometers). A day and night on the moon equals 29 days, 12 hours, and 44 minutes on planet Earth.

NASA

The U.S. National Aeronautics and Space Administration, founded in 1958.

NATIONAL AIR AND SPACE MUSEUM

The largest air and space museum in the United States. Michael Collins was the director between 1971 and 1978.

ORBIT

Circular or elliptical motion—for instance, travel around a planet.

ROCKET

Vehicle powered by fuel according to the reactionary principle. A flow of exhaust fumes (from the fuel) streams out behind the vehicle, thereby propelling the craft forward in the air or in space.

SATURN 5 (also Saturn V)

The launch vehicle for the Apollo spacecraft.

SEA OF TRANQUILITY

Mare Tranquillitatis, one of the "seas," or dark lava plains, on the moon.

SERVICE MODULE

The cylindrical part of Apollo that contained the main spacecraft propulsion system and consumables (oxygen, water, propellants, and hydrogen).

SIMULATOR

Testing device; a mobile replica of the spacecraft or lunar mobile that enables testing maneuvers in advance of actual flight.

SPACE

Extraterrestrial environment.

SPACE RENDEZVOUS

Meeting in space: two spacecraft locating each other and also often docking.

SPACE SICKNESS

A certain kind of motion sickness that can occur in weightlessness, when the nervous system has trouble coordinating perceptions like balance and vision.

SPACE WALK

Work outside the spacecraft.

SPACECRAFT 107

Columbia's serial number.

SPS

Service Propulsion Systems engine, the main engine of the service module.

TEST PILOT

Pilot who tests airplanes under development. In order to be a U.S. test pilot, one has to complete U.S. Air Force or Navy education.

WEIGHTLESSNESS

Lacking apparent gravitational pull.

VACUUM

A space devoid of matter.

The hours and dates in the book refer to the current times at Kennedy Space Center, Florida.

DATE DUE			

629.45
SCH

30118010076812
Schyffert, Bea
Uusma.

The man who went to
the far side of the
moon : the story of
Apollo 11 astronaut

HEYER SCHOOL LIBRARY
WAUKESHA, WISCONSIN   53186

959355 01270   34493C   003